OFFICE OF THE MIDWIFE

Facilitators of the Promise

Nikki Garcia

DEDICATION

This book is dedicated to, firstly, my Lord and Savior Jesus Christ. Thank you for being my friend! Secondly, my husband Alex and beautiful family whom I adore, and lastly, to those who long to "deep sea dive" into the word of God and obtain truth.

FORWARD

I have known the author, Nikki Garcia, for several years because she was a student at The Cleveland Prophetic Institute, affectionately known as "The School of the Prophets."

As a student, Nikki was very thoughtful and reflective in learning the prophetic. She pressed through attending classes as she balanced her work, family, and church life. She has received a mantle to write books and flow in the prophetic, according to her calling as a prophet.

It was with great joy that I read Nikki's book "The Office of the Midwife." Apostle Joseph L. Prude, our founder and Chief Apostle taught us to press into the prophetic, learn the scriptures, and write our visions down.

The midwife is one of the seemingly hidden offices in the church, yet many have found themselves in the place of pushing and assisting others with the birth of their projects and ministries.

In this book, Nikki teaches you how to ease God's people through the birthing projects of their lives and how to guard and nurture the seed produced.

Nikki and I both agree that we are the 'Sons of God' and must take our rightful place and authority on this Earth to bring about God's Kingdom.

I pray that you are edified about the office of the midwife, and how you, too can assist in birthing the things of GOD.

Apostle Denise K. Harris
Dean of The Cleveland Prophetic Institute
East Cleveland, Ohio

TABLE OF CONTENTS

INTRODUCTION

When the Lord spoke to me and told me to write this book, I was initially planning to name it "The Midwife." However, as I began to read and study about the midwife, I came across a scripture that referred to the office of the midwife. I thought to myself, "This is an office?" This discovery was very intriguing to me because I am a dreamer, and I often wondered if there were other offices I might not be aware of in the Bible. I even pondered if being a dreamer was one of them. So, in light of this revelation, I wanted to introduce the Office of the Midwife to some. Our foundational scripture for the office of the midwife can be found in Exodus 1:16 in the KJV.

> *16 and he said: 'When ye do the **office of a midwife** to the Hebrew women, ye shall look upon the birthstool: if it be a son, then ye shall kill him; but if it be a daughter, then she shall live.*

In Hebrew, the word "office of the midwife" is **bə·yal·leḏ·ḵen**.

Usually, when the Bible references the concept of birthing or giving birth, it uses the Hebrew term "yaled," which means to beget. However, this is the only instance in the Bible where the word "bə·yal·led·ḵen" is used, and in its medical context, it refers to the role of a midwife.

In my personal life, on March 4, 2016, I received this word from an Apostle of the Lord where it was declared amongst witnesses that God had declared me as a midwife:

"You are going to write prophetic prayers. That in this dispensation of 5 years I call you a prophetic midwife. You are my midwife. You are my protector and I command you to guard the gates of the women's wombs. You are that person that would push people and say thou shall have this baby. You're going to push this forth. God says that's why you carry people in your dreams. I show you people in your dreams and I take you out in the Spirit. I'm getting ready to carry you away in the Spirit and I'm getting ready to make you this midwife. I know this is going to sound crazy but, you are pregnant with people's wombs. You are to protect their wombs. You are to protect the gates of their wombs. That nothing creeps in and nothing leaks out. I seal you tonight and consecrate you tonight as a midwife in the Spirit. You have a friend you are to carry her in this season that nothing is aborted. Carry those three women that you have been carrying in prayer. I cause them to be your assignment. Your friends, I see you meeting with them. I see a season where God will cause you to start having

prayer in your home, gathering with women just to nurture them."

By this prophetic word by an Apostle of the Lord before witnesses, this office was conferred to me. Let me explain this. According to Authorized Version 1611, the term "office" is defined as:

> A particular duty, charge, or trust conferred by public authority and for a public purpose; an employment undertaken by commission or authority from the government or those who administer it. Thus, we speak of the office of secretary of state, of treasurer, of a judge, of a sheriff, of a justice of the peace, &c. Offices are civil, judicial, ministerial, executive, legislative, political, municipal, diplomatic, military, & ecclesiastical [1]

In the government of God, we are very familiar with the 5-fold officers, which are the apostles, prophets, pastors, evangelists, and teachers. However, we can see from our foundational scripture that other offices exist.

For this role to be considered an office, it must be conferred either politically or ministerially. "Conferred" means to grant or bestow (a title, degree, benefit, or right).

---

[1]c. https://av1611.com/kjbp/kjv-dictionary/office.html

According to the written word and how it describes the role of the midwife, we can equate a midwife as a facilitator. This is the subtitle of this book, "Facilitators of the Promise." A midwife is a person that makes an action or process easy or easier. The goal of the midwife is to bring God's people ease and insight during and through the process of birthing. This person is an earthly vessel facilitating a spiritual result. The midwife acts as a go-between, used to guard the portal that allows the word of God (the seed) to produce a manifested, physical result on Earth.

As you read through this book, it is my prayer that you be enlightened about the Midwife and its office duties in prayer and intercession.

WHO IS THE MIDWIFE?

As intercessors, we have many different places of authority that God teaches us to operate in. If you're not familiar with the ministry of intercession I will do a brief overview.

The focal scripture is Romans 8:33-34

> *33 Who shall lay anything to the charge of God's elect? It is God that justifieth.*
>
> *34 Who is he that condemneth? It is Christ that died, yea rather, that is risen again, who is even at the right hand of God, who also maketh intercession for us.*

This scripture is important because it details what happens in intercession. Let's look at verse 33. It says, "Who shall lay any thing to the charge of God's elect?

Who can say that the elect of God is guilty? The answer is this, Jesus paid the price for sin and as we continue to remain in a place of repentance purification, and sanctification through prayer and the renewal of our minds, our sins are covered under the blood of Jesus. The word of God says, "Love covers a multitude of sins (1 Peter 4:8)". Because of the precious price that Jesus paid, our sins are covered and forgiven. In place of this, I answer that question with a question as Jesus did many times. Who can say that the elect of God is guilty?

Who is the elect of God? The elect are those chosen by God and they are the very ones who have the responsibility of making sure the will of God is accomplished on the earth; they are responsible for the manifestation of the scripture thy Kingdom come and thy will be done.

1 Peter 1:2 KJV

[2] elect according to the foreknowledge of God the Father, through sanctification of the Spirit, unto obedience and sprinkling of the blood of Jesus Christ: Grace unto you, and peace, be multiplied.

Ultimately what this verse is saying is who can condemn whom God has covered?

To top it all off, verse 34 states that Jesus is at the right hand of the Father making intercession for us.

Meaning He pleads our case before God and His blood answers the condemnation that anyone or spirit tries to bring anything against His elect.

This is one of the assignments of Jesus as he dwells at the right hand of the Father. Because of His death, He has the authority to plead our case before God the Father.

In the same way, Jesus has intercessory assignments, we receive intercessory assignments also.

These places of authority are cultivated through a continuous pursuit of God's presence, along with various prayer assignments God would have us complete.

What are "prayer assignments"? These are activities through which we bring petitions and supplications that pertain to His will before the Lord. This includes the many prayers we offer unto the Lord as intermediaries and intercessors who stand in the gap.

Let me give you a less technical description. There are times when God allows me to see things and he speaks to me out of the collective of things He has shown me. I was on Facebook and I saw someone post a picture of the ear. The picture suggested that the ear is a womb. It had a fetus inside of the ear. I thought, "hmmmm that is interesting". I do not totally agree with this because God has expressed to me that earth is a womb (a later chapter in this book) but I do believe that the ear is the place of conception and the womb is the place where what we have heard, grows and matures. We can see this by the Scripture faith cometh by hearing the word of God (Romans 10:17). Later on in the same week, I had a friend that was sharing with me. He began to speak about a word the Lord gave him to release to someone. He said to this person, "Not everyone is a womb for you to release your life issue(s) to."

Between the collective of these two encounters, God began to speak to me. When people come to us with their problems, we have a responsibility as it pertains to what we have heard. We have to be discerning to realize:

(1) Is this an assignment that God is trusting me to carry in my womb?

(2) Is God watching me to see if I would be diligent and accountable as an intercessor? Meaning: Will I be responsible about what I have been entrusted to hear and value that assignment? Will I take this as an opportunity to gossip or will I carry this in prayer until the will of God is manifested concerning the issue?

That is a great assignment and it is just as valuable as the assignment that Jesus has at the right hand of the Father.

INTERCESSION IN MIDWIFERY

If you examine the etymology of the word "midwife":

The word "Midwife" is of Middle English origin, probably derived from the obsolete preposition "*mid*," meaning 'with,' and "*wife*," in the archaic sense 'woman,' expressing the idea of a woman who is with the mother.

Although this definition may suggest that a midwife is a woman, this job is not limited to just women.

My point in exploring the etymology of the midwife is I want you to see that the midwife is with whomever the person is who needs assistance birthing an idea or thought or who is transitioning through a problem. They are with them in the natural providing physical resources and in the spirit taking matters concerning the related issue to the Father.

One thing about God is He is so multifaceted. He has many jobs, and He trains us in the varying capacities that He operates in. As we are faithful and keep showing up, He entrusts us with more to cultivate and birth forth on the Earth. He uses our wombs to be great producers. The ability to be birthers is not limited to women only (as I mentioned earlier); it is an ability given by God to be able to function as He does because we are made in His image and likeness.

As Christians, we see examples of the Office of the Midwife as God reveals Himself in the word as the *"I am"* God to Moses. Moses asked the Lord, who should I tell your people sent me? God told Moses to say, *"I Am,"* which translates to *"God is."* He is whatever is needed at any given time. So, we can see from this example that God used Moses as a midwife to bring His people out of exile.

This is also illustrated in Numbers 11:12 based on the analogy Moses presents to God about the children of Israel who wanted meat to eat.

> **12** *Have I conceived all this people? have I begotten them, that thou shouldest say unto me, Carry them in thy bosom, as a nursing father beareth the sucking child, unto the land which thou swarest unto their fathers?*

In other words, Moses says to God (paraphrased), "Listen, these are your people, but you are requiring me to nurse them. You want me to be a nursing father to these children until they come into the land of promise." This is an illustration of how God used Moses, a man, to birth and facilitate the promise.

The Office of the Midwife is not just for women but also for men. It is about the manifestation of God's will for the Earth.

In my personal life, God has given me prophetic words to be a midwife to certain people. The assignment was to carry them until they came into a greater knowledge of who God is and until they came into the fulfillment of certain plans and promises for their lives.

An example assignment involved a close friend facing the daunting challenges of a lupus diagnosis, compounded by medication effects on her kidneys. After praying and praying and not being healed, she had come to a place where she felt, in her exact words, "She was going to take her salvation and move on". She had lost all hope. At this critical juncture, it was an emergency not to abandon someone in a state of hopelessness. This particular friend became one of my assigned responsibilities, and the experience highlighted the transformative power of intercessory prayer, the significance of unwavering encouragement in moments of despair, and the profound responsibility of representing God's love.

There are times when you may even need an assistant in some cases. Even in birthing rooms, the doctors have assistance. I called another skilled midwife to assist and this midwife would pastor her for years. With both of our midwifery skills, this friend is now in a greater place of faith and able to believe and trust God as she walks out her healing.

In summary, Midwives stand as legal Guardians of transport and act as representatives of the Kingdom of God that has given a thing the divine approval to enter the earth. What does all that mean? It means the role of the midwife is to be a facilitator. A facilitator is a person that makes an action or process easy or easier. The goal of the midwife is to bring God's people ease and insight during and through the process of birth. That makes this person an earthly vessel facilitating a spiritual result as I mentioned earlier. Midwives occupy the gate of a portal and they dictate what can come in and what stays out. In essence, a midwife is a protector. We will explore this in the next chapter.

Yalad in the Bible means to beget but it also has a definition that means travail. Travail means to bring something from one place of being into another place of being so midwifery is the ministry of transport.

If you would like to learn more about intercession, you can preorder my soon-to-be-released book, The Answer to Prayer.

WHAT IS THE MIDWIFE'S JOB DESCRIPTION?
THE GIFT OF THE MIDWIFE

UNDERSTANDING THE GIFT

Have you ever seen a child and that child was gifted? When they come into this world they already come with abilities. These abilities just operate without any character development, processing, maturity, responsibility, faithfulness, servitude, or effort. They are just gifted at some particular thing. Whether that thing is sports, music, supernatural insight, intelligence, or superior comprehension, this child operates in their gifting above the common level of operation.

This is what a gift looks like. A gift is about function. It is about how a thing operates. The Bible says that the gifts and callings are without repentance (Romans 11:29). Let's review 1 Samuel 3:3-20

> *3 And the child Samuel ministered unto the Lord before Eli. And the word of the Lord was precious in those days; there was no open vision.*
>
> *2 And it came to pass at that time, when Eli was laid down in his place, and his eyes began to wax dim, that he could not see;*
>
> *3 And ere the lamp of God went out in the temple of the Lord, where the ark of God was, and Samuel was laid down to sleep;*

4 That the Lord called Samuel: and he answered, Here am I.

5 And he ran unto Eli, and said, Here am I; for thou calledst me. And he said, I called not; lie down again. And he went and lay down.

6 And the Lord called yet again, Samuel. And Samuel arose and went to Eli, and said, Here am I; for thou didst call me. And he answered, I called not, my son; lie down again.

7 Now Samuel did not yet know the Lord, neither was the word of the Lord yet revealed unto him.

8 And the Lord called Samuel again the third time. And he arose and went to Eli, and said, Here am I; for thou didst call me. And Eli perceived that the Lord had called the child.

9 Therefore Eli said unto Samuel, Go, lie down: and it shall be, if he call thee, that thou shalt say, Speak, Lord; for thy servant heareth. So Samuel went and lay down in his place.

10 And the Lord came, and stood, and called as at other times, Samuel, Samuel. Then Samuel answered, Speak; for thy servant heareth.

11 And the Lord said to Samuel, Behold, I will do a thing in Israel, at which both the ears of every one that heareth it shall tingle.

12 In that day I will perform against Eli all things which I have spoken concerning his house: when I begin, I will also make an end.

13 For I have told him that I will judge his house for ever for the iniquity which he knoweth; because his sons made themselves vile, and he restrained them not.

14 And therefore I have sworn unto the house of Eli, that the iniquity of Eli's house shall not be purged with sacrifice nor offering for ever.

15 And Samuel lay until the morning, and opened the doors of the house of the Lord. And Samuel feared to shew Eli the vision.

16 Then Eli called Samuel, and said, Samuel, my son. And he answered, Here am I.

17 And he said, What is the thing that the Lord hath said unto thee? I pray thee hide it not from me: God do so to thee, and more also, if thou hide any thing from me of all the things that he said unto thee.

18 And Samuel told him every whit, and hid nothing from him. And he said, It is the Lord: let him do what seemeth him good.

19 And Samuel grew, and the Lord was with him, and did let none of his words fall to the ground.

20 And all Israel from Dan even to Beersheba knew that Samuel was established to be a prophet of the Lord.

Now first and foremost being someone who occupies an office is not an event that just happens. There was a process and it was established, inaugural, by the word of God.

What is inaugural?

Marking the beginning of an institution, activity, or period of office.

Let's note 3 things:

- Samuel grew (there was a process; a process of growing)
- The Lord was with Him (God was with Him in the process of growth)
- He let none of his words fall to the ground (God established him, in his region, by not allowing any of his words fall to the ground)

Reiterating verse 20, Samuel was established, there was a jurisdiction that he operated in regionally, and in that jurisdiction, all knew him because of the fruit that he yielded. He was activated and inaugurated to be a prophet of the Lord with an assignment in the region he resided in. In the Bible, there was an end to one priestly regime and then God invoked a new priestly regime and backed it with the affirming of His word.

In comparison, the same goes for Midwives Puah and Shiphrah; they were the Hebrew midwives. Now the unique thing about these Egyptian Midwives, some tradition suggests that they were not Hebrew but they were allowed to deliver Hebrew babies. This was strictly a no-go because the Hebrews believed that outside midwives would kill their children but in this instance, they were "adopted" midwives.

Because they feared the Lord they disobeyed the command from Pharaoh to kill the Hebrew babies

To summarize the gift typically operates person to person.

THE JOB DESCRIPTION

As we further delve into this section, let's first define what a dimension is. A dimension is the dichotomy of man. It is the ability of man to be in this world but not of this world. It is man's ability to be dimensional. An example of this would be how man has dominion on Earth but is seated in heavenly places with Christ Jesus (Eph 2:6). We also see this in the makeup of man. Man is a three-part being: body, soul, and spirit. By his spirit, he can interact in the unseen realm while existing physically in the natural world.

The Ministry of Transport

I had a dream, and in a part of this dream, I had a revelation or just instantaneous knowledge about a dimension. Dimensions have gateways, and they are what you use to bring something from one dimension into another. An example of this knowledge is Earth (the dimension in which we reside); to bring something back from Heaven (a dimension), you need a gateway. As the dream continued, I saw a gateway that opened, allowing me to put my hand in it and transport myself from one dimension to another. We see this same example in the natural world, as when a woman has a child, her vagina serves as a gateway, and the doctor may use their hands to assist with the baby's delivery into the natural world. God began to elaborate on this scenario even more by directing me to John 6:16-21.

16 And when evening was now come, his disciples went down unto the sea, 17 And entered into a ship, and went over the sea toward Capernaum. And it was now dark, and Jesus was not come to them. 18 And the sea arose by reason of a great wind that blew. 19 So when they had rowed about five and twenty or thirty furlongs, they see Jesus walking on the sea, and drawing nigh unto the ship:

and they were afraid. 20 But he saith unto them, It is I; be not afraid. 21 Then they willingly received him into the ship: and immediately the ship was at the land whither they went.

What we see from the passage above is that Jesus' disciples were on the sea. The sea rose due to a strong wind blowing. The disciples rowed approximately 3.125 to 3.75 miles, and they saw Jesus walking on the sea. They received Him into the ship, and immediately, it was **transported** to the land. In verse 19, **they transitioned** from the dimension of man to the dimension of the spirit in verse 21 when they received Jesus into the boat and were teleported to land. Jesus was the gateway into the Spirit, and once they received Him, they were teleported. A spiritual result was born. Jesus was the gateway that allowed them to operate in another place of authority. We can see Jesus' authority as we observe from the scripture, that when He came to the disciples, He was walking on water. This was an aspect of authority that they had not operated in or previously experienced. A midwife, operating with greater authority, can be the conduit that stands as the gateway that assists you in birthing the new dimension of authority that you are now meant to operate in.

The Midwife, The Warrior

The midwife is a term I coined as the "hand warrior". What do I mean when I say this? The Bible says that He teaches our hands to war and our fingers to fight.

Psalms 144:1

A Psalm of David. Blessed be the LORD my strength, which teacheth my hands to war, and my fingers to fight

The midwife's role and job duties (which are the works of their hands), wage war in both spiritual and natural realms to bring about the manifestation of God's will. Their hands represent the hand of God and what this person touches is indicative of how the doctor may at times use their hands to assist with delivery. The hand, in this case, is God's hand literally pulling a thing out of the spirit into the natural through their watch care. The midwife remains with the individual(s) pregnant with God's intellectual property which is His divine will for matters and purposes on earth.

The midwife's work and job duties are outlined below.

To Protect

Midwives have one of the most important jobs because being a midwife essentially is about safeguarding the seed. God places people in position to watch over the seed that He implants in your womb. God is deeply concerned with the birth of His seed. We see this in the lineage of Jesus Christ. God needed a righteous lineage to come through, and if you trace the lineage of Jesus Christ, you will observe this.

During various midwifery assignments, God would have me uphold the who or the what in prayer. As I entered into intercession God would give me insight concerning His will for the individuals and it allowed me to minister to their place of need. The intercession was necessary to be able to see into their life as God would allow so that I could minister the will of God concerning their growth.

To Guard

A midwife stands as a guardian. This individual protects the seed from abortion and premature delivery, guides the mother/father to preserve their life, and addresses all the care, questions, and concerns related to watchful care.

To Undergird

The Midwife is an exemplary of an undergirding intercessor. In the natural world, when a woman conceives a child, in times past, a midwife was needed to assist with the delivery of an unborn child.

The midwife would provide answers to questions, offer words of encouragement, and oversee the overall health of the pregnancy. In modern times, a midwife might resemble an OBGYN or a coach. Coaches are often enlisted to help you transition from one stage of your life to another. They facilitate growth and "produce" in the Earth.

The Midwife actively participates in the process of transition or the birth of a child. They don't merely stand by with "yes" and "amen"; they provide exercises and encouragement and maintain constant, fervent interaction with the process.

This is what undergirding looks like in the spirit. It is not to stand there with your hands folded or to just come into agreement with the prayer. It is active and willful participation in the prayer with tongues, travail, agreement, and demonstration.

I had a friend that would show up and disappear many times in my life. God revealed to me that those times when she would come back for those short periods were midwifery. She needed encouragement, undergirding, direction, and guidance. Once that occurred she would be able to manage and advance her life and sometimes that is all that is required.

To Worship & Revere God

The midwife understands the need to have the reverential fear of God. This person understands what has to be birthed is the will of God, the word, the thoughts, and the plans of God. This person is a keeper of His intellectual property and understands that they work as His handmaiden to establish His works on Earth. How do I know this? Because Jeremiah 29:11 states *For I know the plans I have for you,' declares the Lord, 'plans to prosper you and not to harm you, plans to give you a hope and a future.*

We also see this explicitly with midwives Shiphrah and Puah. They were Hebrew midwives, and because they feared God, they would not kill the Hebrew boys as Pharaoh had commanded. We read this in Exodus 1:15-21.

> *15 And the king of Egypt spake to the Hebrew midwives, of which the name of the one was Shiphrah, and the name of the other Puah:*
>
> *16 And he said, When ye do the office of a midwife to the Hebrew women, and see them upon the stools; if it be a son, then ye shall kill him: but if it be a daughter, then she shall live.*

17 But the midwives feared God, and did not as the king of Egypt commanded them, but saved the men children alive.

18 And the king of Egypt called for the midwives, and said unto them, Why have ye done this thing, and have saved the men children alive?

19 And the midwives said unto Pharaoh, Because the Hebrew women are not as the Egyptian women; for they are lively, and are delivered ere the midwives come in unto them.

These two women would be considered activists today. They came up with a plan to go against politics. They defied the law of the king out of reverence for God, and God established their households because of this manner of reverence.

Something to also note is that God used two midwives. The number two is so significant in the Bible. It often means the confirmation and the establishment of God's word.

There are times as a midwife God will use your worship, reverence, and fear of Him to bring others into an increased level of worship, reverence, and fear of God. He will birth this in them because it is a capacity that the midwife functions in. I have a friend, whom I love, that needed a lot of assistance. At that time, she was living with her boyfriend, involved in addictive practices, in and out of being a stripper, she had a baby at a young age and was constantly in financial need. I supported her in many ways naturally and spiritually but there wasn't a change in her mind about her sinful lifestyle. Eventually, we had a very confrontative conversation about her life decisions. It was a yelling match but we both heard each other. We lost contact because financially she couldn't maintain a phone. A good amount of time passed between me being actively engaged in her life and she reached out to me and apologized and she repented to God and me. She was ready to make a change in her life. Her eyes began to see the truth in the things I was trying to convey in that strong conversation. She expressed how she wanted change and wanted me back in her life. It was a pouring out of repentance before God. Our interactions of love, even in strong conversations, birthed true repentance and change in her life.

To Comfort

As I was on a podcast, The Marketplace Pastor, and I was given questions to answer concerning this book. The host asked me, "What is the difference between a coach and a midwife?" This was a very good question. One that I had not even thought to convey.

As I asked the Holy Spirit what was the difference, this is what He told me. With a coach, there will be a set of tasks or challenges, and related or desired goals with corresponding outcomes that will improve one's skillfulness.

Going back to the etymology of the word midwife, this person is "with" the woman. "With" is the operative word. Think of God "*with*" us. God walked "*with*" Adam in the cool of the day. Now Jesus walked "with" the disciples and He would say to them periodically when they were faithless or doubtful, "How long will I be *with* thee". Let's read John 14:12-17.

> *12 Verily, verily, I say unto you, He that believeth on me, the works that I do shall he do also; and greater works than these shall he do; because I go unto my Father.*
>
> *13 And whatsoever ye shall ask in my name, that will I do, that the Father may be glorified in the Son.*
>
> *14 If ye shall ask any thing in my name, I will do it.*
>
> *15 If ye love me, keep my commandments.*
>
> *16 And I will pray the Father, and he shall give you another* **Comforter,** *that he may abide* **with** *you for ever;*
>
> *17 Even the Spirit of truth; whom the world cannot receive, because it seeth him not, neither knoweth him: but ye know him; for he dwelleth* **with** *you, and shall be* **in** *you.*
>
> *18 I will not leave you* **comfortless** *I will come to you*

There are different points I want to bring out and they are detailed below:

(1) The Holy Spirit is a midwife. How so? He is with us and with us through eternity according to Scripture. He comes with encouragement, instruction, wisdom, leading, all manner of understanding, and blueprints for God's will to be accomplished on the earth. How does He do this? He accomplishes this through our ability to receive the baptism of the Holy Ghost and fire. The Bible says that the Holy Spirit will make intercession through us with moanings and groanings that can not be uttered (Romans 8:26). We have Jesus, the Son of God, sitting at the right hand of the Father making intercession for us (Romans 8:34). We have the Holy Spirit dwelling on the inside of us making intercession through us. This is why we speak in tongues and this is one of the reasons why speaking in an unknown tongue is so necessary. That the Holy Spirit can do the work of midwifery that we know him and come into the image of Him.

(2) Let's observe v. 16, Jesus prayed to the Father and this prayer was to give us another comforter. Jesus was the comforter that walked with us but the Holy Spirit is the comforter that dwells within us. That is one of the names of the Holy Spirit (John 16:7). The Holy Spirit is the one that brings us a future and a hope. It is through this person of

the Godhead that we are comforted when we go through various tests and trials.

(3) One last point I want to express, the Midwives, Shiphrah and Puah, according to Rabbinical text, documented in the Jewish Women Archives, had different jobs that they did as they operated in their office. Shiprah would clean the baby off after birth (*Shiphrah: Midrash and Aggadah*, n.d.). Puah would wail with the woman when she wailed and that was known to bring comfort (*Puah: Midrash and Aggadah*, n.d.). This parallels some of the jobs of the Holy Spirit. He cleans us up with the fire and refines us. Just Shiprah when she cleaned the after birth and Puah would wail and bring comfort just as the Holy Ghost does for us.

To Facilitate Multiplicity

Exodus 1:20-21

> *20 Therefore God dealt well with the midwives: and the people multiplied, and waxed very mighty.*
>
> *21 And it came to pass, because the midwives feared God, that he made them houses.*

In the book of Genesis, God promised to bless Abraham and we are all partakers of the blessing that comes from God's promises. We are blessed to multiply and just as the scriptures above reinforced, God blessed the work of the midwives' hands. He blessed their work because they pleased Him and He caused their operation on the earth to facilitate His promise to multiply.

Practically, there are many ways these functions can be executed. There are times when the Lord will use the Midwife to be the one that assists people in their transitory places whereby the midwife would have to carry someone for just a short time. Sometimes they will just need you to get past a challenging scenario in their life. Other times the assignment can be arduous and/or long lasting. An example of this was a former coworker of mine who went through a divorce. I stayed with this individual with encouragement, prophetic words, and dreams from the Lord which gave insight into their situation, words of knowledge, and wisdom. Once this person got past their divorce and remarried our relationship changed. This was not because of anything I did or they did, it was just I was there to help this person through their divorce into a new beginning in life. I was also even able to bring this person to Christ through this short time of midwifery. This type of midwifery facilitated multiplication because a baby came out of this marriage.

In summary, the gift is the function that ineptly operates in our lives. We are born with a gift and we function within that gift. In the case of a midwife, this would be someone who just takes on clients one by one and assists them as I mentioned earlier. They will handle individualistic assignments.

But an officer is typically established by the word of God, given assignments within His Kingdom, and one who produces jurisdictionally under the governance of God. An officer's assignment(s) would be to the body. How do I know this? Let's look at Ephesians 4:11-12

> *[11] And he gave some, apostles; and some, prophets; and some, evangelists; and some, pastors and teachers; [12] for the perfecting of the saints, for the work of the ministry, for the edifying of the body of Christ:*

The officers are for the work of the ministry and the edifying of the body of Christ.

The word *work* in Ephesians 4:12 is rgon in the Greek. Its usage is as follows: work, task, employment; a deed, action; that which is wrought or made, a work.

2041 érgon (from ergō, "to work, accomplish") – a work or worker who accomplishes something. 2041 /érgon ("work") is a deed (action) that carries out (completes) an inner desire (intension, purpose).

In essence, God hires you for the work of the ministry, for some task. When He hires you for ministry, He gives you the mind to serve.

The word *ministry* in Ephesians 4:12 means:

c. of the ministration or service of all who, endowed by God with powers of mind and heart peculiarly adapted to this end, endeavor zealously and laboriously to promote the cause of Christ among men, as apostles, prophets, evangelists, elders, etc

Referring back to Samuel, he was established as a prophet to take Eli's place. In the case of Puah and Shiphrah, they saved the future of a nation of people. Because they feared God and saved a future generation. They were midwives to a generation and their assignment was to save the established government of God in the earth and this is why they were in the office. It wasn't just about a gift or skill but about the fact that they were established to preserve, protect and guard the nation of people that God was using on the earth symbolically as the government of God.

At first, as God is with you and grows and matures you and your character, He gives you individual assignments to grow you. To actuate produce within the gift but eventually, it goes wider than relationally and extends into jurisdictionally.

HOW DOES THE MIDWIFE EXECUTE THE PLAN OF GOD?

THE OFFICE AND ITS JUDICIAL ASSIGNMENT

AN OBSERVATION OF A JURISDICTIONAL ASSIGNMENT FOR THE BODY

One morning, when I awoke for prayer, God began to tell me that Deborah was a midwife in the Bible. I responded, "Really?" and proceeded to search the Bible to find references to Deborah. I knew her to be a prophet and a judge, but I was unaware of her being a midwife. As I began to read Judges chapter 5, I came across verse 7, which stated the following:

> *7 The inhabitants of the villages ceased, they ceased in Israel, until that I Deborah arose, that I arose a mother in Israel.*

I was amazed to see this. Deborah was a mother in Israel. In this instance, mother, according to Strong's bible concordance, means a mother caring for her people.

As I was driving in my car, God began to speak to me about this story. You have Barak, whom Deborah called to herself and gave him the word of the Lord, telling him that God was instructing him to go to war against Sisera, the commander of Jabin's army. This is detailed in **Judges 4:6-11.**

6 And she sent and called Barak the son of Abinoam out of Kedeshnaphtali, and said unto him, Hath not the Lord God of Israel commanded, saying, Go and draw toward mount Tabor, and take with thee ten thousand men of the children of Naphtali and of the children of Zebulun?

7 And I will draw unto thee to the river Kishon Sisera, the captain of Jabin's army, with his chariots and his multitude; and I will deliver him into thine hand.

8 And Barak said unto her, If thou wilt go with me, then I will go: but if thou wilt not go with me, then I will not go.

9 And she said, I will surely go with thee: notwithstanding the journey that thou takest shall not be for thine honour; for the Lord shall sell Sisera into the hand of a woman. And Deborah arose, and went with Barak to Kedesh.

10 And Barak called Zebulun and Naphtali to Kedesh; and he went up with ten thousand men at his feet: and Deborah went up with him.

11 Now Heber the Kenite, which was of the children of Hobab the father in law of Moses, had severed himself from the Kenites, and pitched his tent unto the plain of Zaanaim, which is by Kedesh.

This passage shows that Deborah was a protector of God's intellectual property. It was the will of God to rescue His people. God sent for Barak through His prophet, Deborah. She gave him the word of God to go and pursue, and he would overtake. He didn't want to overtake Sisera (the Canaanite general) without Deborah. Deborah responds to him and says (paraphrased), "I will go with you despite the journey, but you won't get this honor. Sisera will be given over into a woman's hands." Either way, God used whomever He needed to rescue His people. So after Jabin (the king of the Canaanites) was captured, the song of the Lord came forth. Deborah and Barak rejoiced in a song about their recount of victory.

Judges 4:12

> *12 Awake, awake, Deborah: awake, awake, utter a song: arise, Barak, and lead thy captivity captive, thou son of Abinoam.*

Let's delve into verse 12 and focus on some important points.

(1) The word "awake" in verse 12 means to get into gear. This is similar to how your child may be perfectly fine sitting on the couch, and then you see them heading towards the

pool. You would awaken out of a lax place into a place of alertness and guarding.

(2) We can see from verse 12 that God is calling Deborah and saying I am summoning you for work. According to Judges 4:5, Amplified Bible, *She used to sit [to hear and decide disputes] under the palm tree of Deborah between Ramah and Bethel in the hill country of Ephraim; and the Israelites came up to her for judgment.*

(3) God says to her, "Utter a song: arise, Barak, and lead thy captivity captive, thou son of Abinoam." The assignment He gave her was an assignment which was to worship, which is a dimension of service akin to the midwife that we mentioned earlier.

Then God summons Barak through the direction He gave Deborah to give to him, and he tells him to gather an army that will take captives. Barak goes to Deborah to receive the counsel of God, which gives him God's judicial approval. Let's talk about God's Judicial Approval and what that is. Let's gain insight about God's Judicial Approval by looking at Matthew 6:33.

Seek ye first the kingdom of God and all of His righteousness and all things will be added unto you.

This scripture in Greek was broken down like this...Inquire (investigate, look into) FIRST of God's government, His authority, His sovereignty, and rule concerning His **judicial approval,** and each and everything, all parts included, "the whole" will be added unto you.

When you receive the word of the Lord, it is God giving you the authority to do a thing, and from that thing, every benefit or promise associated with it will be added unto you. Once Barak gets the word (judicial approval) from Deborah to do this thing, he says to her, "I won't go without you." Meaning it isn't good enough to just be pregnant with the word of God, to hear the prophetic word and receive it. But as I go forth, I need you to be a midwife to help me care for the word that you released over my life. Deborah was a gatekeeper. During this time, the warriors became fat and sloppy, meaning they were no longer prepared to wage war. They had become out of shape. They no longer could sustain blows or issue them, for that matter. This is seen in Judges 5:7.

> 7 Warriors became fat and sloppy, no fight left in them.
> Then you, Deborah, rose up; you got up, a mother in Israel.

Every time a person didn't keep the word of God in the Bible and did not follow His commands, He would always raise up a person or people who would.

An example of this is Eli and Samuel. I spoke about this earlier. When Eli's eyes waxed dim and he allowed his sons to take the fat of the sacrifices and the women that came to the temple, God became angry because he did not rebuke his sons. God raised up Samuel. In the word, He says that He would raise up a faithful priest.

In the case of Deborah, here arose a gatekeeper, Deborah, who never lost her strength, and she continued to occupy the gates. God chose a new leader to fight at the gates.

I am a web developer and graphic designer and on the mountain of business, I am constantly giving people the word of the Lord and helping them to facilitate the promise of God. I operate as a gatekeeper of the ideas God wants to birth in the marketplace. I had one particular client who came to me and wasn't sure which way to go with their business. We had our initial consultation and I prophecied what her business is and the direction she should go in. She replied, "That's exactly what I want to do. You articulated what I couldn't." From the word of the Lord, we brought an entity from being on the mind of God into being an established entity on earth. We legislated the will and mind of God concerning business in the earthly realm.

In summary, the Midwife executes the plan of God by the following:

(1) Upholding their job description. They are going to execute the plan of God by doing the 5 jobs I mentioned earlier in the book which are: to protect, guard, undergird, worship and revere, and facilitate multiplication.

(2) Just as a midwife in the natural realm gives guidance, the midwife gives guidance and this guidance is the counsel of the Lord concerning the mind and will of God. This counsel is the judicial approval, the authority, from God, for a thing to be established under His government.

(3) The midwife will worship God as the mind and will of God is birthed forth on earth.

(4) Watching is very imperative to the execution of the will of God being manifested on earth. Watching includes being on guard, being alert, being properly postured, being activated, and staying activated through the course of the operation.

(5) Delivering the promise: You must stay in a place of belief and wage war with any obstacle that will try to bring diversions. Delivering the promise includes: TRAVAIL: Which includes constant and fervent action to engage the spirit to push the thought and will of God from one dimension to the next.

WHY DO WE NEED THE MIDWIFE'S ASSISTANCE?

The reason we need midwives is that they preserve legacy. They are the facilitator of the promise.

We see the preservation of legacy through the story of Ruth. Ruth was a midwife for Israel. God utilized Ruth's womb to continue the righteous bloodline of Jesus Christ. He used Ruth's womb so that the generational bloodline would not be cut off. Also, Ruth's son, Obed, begot Jesse, and Jesse begot David, who was a king and a fighter for Israel. The elders prayed over Ruth's seed.

> *10 Moreover Ruth the Moabitess, the wife of Mahlon, have I purchased to be my wife, to raise up the name of the dead upon his inheritance, that the name of the dead be not cut off from among his brethren, and from the gate of his place: ye are witnesses this day.*
>
> *11 And all the people that were in the gate, and the elders, said, We are witnesses. The Lord make the woman that is come into thine house like Rachel and like Leah, which two did build the house of Israel: and do thou worthily in Ephratah, and be famous in Bethlehem:*
>
> *12 And let thy house be like the house of Pharez, whom Tamar bare unto Judah, of the seed which the Lord shall give thee of this young woman.*

Through Ruth, Israel was later redeemed by her great-grandson David, who defeated the giants in the land.

What is awesome about this is that you have all of these men who take counsel together. They stand at the city gates about the land and the generational inheritance of Naomi's husband. They stood at the gates to decide what manner of recompense was due, and based on everyone's current status and situation, the inheritance was dealt appropriately. God used a Moabite woman to preserve this God nation of Israel. It was a foreshadowing of the type that neither Greek nor Jew.... Galatians 3:28

EARTH IS A WOMB

When I was in prayer recently, I heard God tell me that Earth is a womb.

He began to express to me a popularly quoted scripture,

> *Psalms 24:1 - The Earth is the LORD'S, and the fullness of it, the world, and those who dwell in it.*

Follow this thought with me. The book of Genesis declares that the Earth was full of water. If we read in the book of Genesis 1:7, God said he divided the waters from the waters.

> *7 And God made the firmament, and divided the waters which were under the firmament from the waters which were above the firmament: and it was so.*

In science, it is declared that the earth is 71% water and 29% land.

When a woman becomes pregnant, the womb is filled with amniotic fluid: water, electrolytes, and minerals. A woman gives birth out of the waters.

One of the most beautiful parallelisms of the womb, to me, is the Garden of Eden. Why? Because it was a place that God birthed, created and established.

Let's review some of the attributes of the womb:

Natural parallelism - Spiritual parallelism

It is the place of Intimacy - Worship

It is the place of conception - Fertilization of the egg with sperm

It is the place of the transference of DNA - Information (revealed knowledge)

Billowing into the uterus and protected encasement - It is the place of growth and maturation (the place of dwelling and hiding)

It is the place of being born - Born again

From these attributes of the womb, God began to reveal to me that the womb was a watch. Adam's watch was the garden but Eve's watch was the womb.

She is a "WOMB-MAN." She is the one that conceives.

To confirm this revealing in the Bible, the judgments that were rendered revealed the transgression against God's word.

> *Genesis 3:14-21*
>
> *14 Then the Lord God said to the snake, "You will be punished for this; you alone of all the animals must bear this curse: From now on you will crawl on your belly, and you*

will have to eat dust as long as you live. 15 I will make you and the woman hate each other; her offspring and yours will always be enemies. Her offspring will crush your head, and you will bite her offspring's[a] heel."

16 And he said to the woman, "I will increase your trouble in pregnancy and your pain in giving birth. In spite of this, you will still have desire for your husband, yet you will be subject to him."

17 And he said to the man, "You listened to your wife and ate the fruit which I told you not to eat. Because of what you have done, the ground will be under a curse. You will have to work hard all your life to make it produce enough food for you. 18 It will produce weeds and thorns, and you will have to eat wild plants. 19 You will have to work hard and sweat to make the soil produce anything, until you go back to the soil from which you were formed. You were made from soil, and you will become soil again."

Earth is the womb of God. In the womb, there is transference of DNA from the Father. DNA only comes from the Father. This is exactly what happened in the Garden of Eden when God created man.

This is seen in the Bible when God spoke and God breathed Himself into man he became a living soul (Genesis 1:26-29)

26 And God said, Let us make man in our image, after our likeness: and let them have dominion over the fish of the sea, and over the fowl of the air, and over the cattle, and over all the earth, and over every creeping thing that creepeth upon the earth.

27 So God created man in his own image, in the image of God created he him; male and female created he them.

28 And God blessed them, and God said unto them, Be fruitful, and multiply, and replenish the earth, and subdue it: and have dominion over the fish of the sea, and over the fowl of the air, and over every living thing that moveth upon the earth.

29 And God said, Behold, I have given you every herb bearing seed, which is upon the face of all the earth, and every tree, in the which is the fruit of a tree yielding seed; to you it shall be for meat.

Adam and Eve could be considered a type of midwife whose job was post-care. They were to maintain that which God had birthed. If we examine man and his function and purpose, we can see this is still our job today though many of us don't always have a clear view of any aspect of our purpose as created beings on earth let alone to understand the necessity of earth's guardianship.

We must continue to speak the word of God over those things He has given us. This is also a part of our intercessory duties that we transfer the DNA of God where things have become corrupt and that we guard, protect, and allow God's mind and will for us to grow and mature.

The Bible declares, "that thy Kingdom come and thy will be done on earth as it is in heaven." With a basic understanding of creation, we see that God intended Earth to be a replica of Heaven. The objective of man was to manage and maintain the order that God had already established. We see this in Genesis, where the word of God says the Earth was void and without form. God entered this place of darkness and lack of order and firstly established His glory (light) and, secondly, established order under Him. Once God created everything, He placed man here to manage what He had established. Man's management was always meant to come out of a relationship with God. Just as God walked with Adam in the cool of the day, there was a partnership in rulership. When we are outside of that partnership with God, the womb of Earth cannot exhibit the replication of Heaven. Let's read Romans 8:19-22 to get an understanding.

> *19 For the earnest expectation of the creature waiteth for the manifestation of the sons of God.*

20 For the creature was made subject to vanity, not willingly, but by reason of him who hath subjected the same in hope,

21 Because the creature itself also shall be delivered from the bondage of corruption into the glorious liberty of the children of God.

22 For we know that the whole creation groaneth and travaileth in pain together until now.

If you look at the current state of the world and the Ekklesia, you can see the lack of rulership from the creature (man).

Sidenote: most scriptures speak about God's creation as creatures and beings. Whether it be angels, man, animals, or whatever He created.

Because we are not witnessing the power of God, the Kingship of God through man, many people feel as if God doesn't exist. If you talk to some atheists, a significant reason for their atheism is their lack of concrete evidence that God is who the Bible declares Him to be.

With that being said, the Earth travails, which means it experiences storms, tornadoes, irregular weather, shifts in its axis, and a slower rotation. All of these signs are indicative of a problem on Earth, and the problem isn't with the physical Earth itself; they are signs of the condition of man (Earth). As long as man (the womb) is not in his rightful place of authority and ruling from his kingly position in relationship with God, then the Earth (the womb) cannot be the exact replica of Heaven as God intended it to be.

THE MIDWIFE, THE MOUTH AND ITS FUNCTION

THE OFFICE AND ITS LEGISLATION

Now that we understand that Earth is a womb, we can comprehend how we use this Earth suit and its various functions to legislate God's will here on Earth.

Midwives have the responsibility to guard the gates of the womb. The womb indicates how God chooses to mature the blessing before it manifests in the earthly realm. As spiritual guards, the midwife must be confident that everything spoken from his/her mouth will bring forth the word of faith.

The mouth is one of the most important gates that we possess. The mouth is the very thing that allows us to express the inherent power (The Holy Spirit) that lives within us. Through the canal of the mouth, a couple of things happen. (1) We have the ability for intake, and (2) we have the ability for outtake. Predominantly, we use the canal of our mouth for outward expression of what is going on inwardly. The Bible states this specifically out of the abundance of the heart the mouth speaks.

With that being said, we want to tap into the ability of the midwife's mouth to be the womb to the abundance of vision for those that they carry.

One thing you will see in prayer is that the Earth's womb is idle until someone invokes it with the spirit. This is seen in one of the midwife's inherent abilities to speak forth, and as they speak forth in the spirit, the DNA of God is transferred into another's assignment. They can bring clarity and understanding on how to walk processes out. Their job is to bring their knowledge and wisdom to the scenario so that proper information is gathered to accomplish goals. The midwives job is to bring you to the place of PUSH. Everything that they assist you with will facilitate the birthing of this "new" thing.

A personal experience of this is my husband had received the word a few times about a promotion coming to him. The first thing God had me to do was fast from 9-5. He told me to do this because he wanted to double our income. My husband and I fasted and prayed one week together and I fasted and prayed alone for 2 weeks. He had a review coming up and they gave him a $20,000 raise. Though this was great, it was not the magnitude that our household needed. We began looking for other jobs because we felt the increase would come that way. A lot of offers came in but none met the magnitude of our need.

The next fast God had me to do was fasting from 10 am - 12 pm. At this time I was pregnant and I shared my concern with God concerning fasting while pregnant. I was making a plea saying,

"Lord that is a lot right not because I am hungry with this baby". His reply was, "This fast is not about eating as it is more about your obedience. I want you to pray for two hours every day". Now of course this was on top of my regular prayer time but it was fine. So for a couple of weeks, I would get on my piano and pray and worship God and speak over our finances and use my mouth to declare the word and confess His word.

My husband received an offer with the DOD and we were getting geared up to go to Maryland but there were all manner of checks and balances that had to occur because of the level of security needed to work for the DOD. One of those checks and balances was that they would need to speak to my husband's current employer. We both were like, "Whoa" but, my husband finally let his boss know and his boss said, "Congratulations. I can't compete with that but I can meet their offer and beat that offer". My husband told him what they were offering and his boss met that offer plus he went $10,000 over their offer. In 4 months, God blessed our home with $60,000. It was God's will to double our income and He used my mouth and obedience to push His will on the earth.

Some of the very scriptures I prayed are prayers in this book and you can use those prayers to allow your mouth to be a womb for God.

PRAYERS FOR MIDWIVES AND BIRTHERS

I pray that no seed ever placed in my care will die a sudden death, be aborted, or be contaminated by outside forces or influences.

I bind all demonic watchers that lie in wait as the seed I have watched over is transported from the unseen realm to the seen realm.

I pray that my guardianship is backed by the angelic forces that will wage war as I contend in righteousness for the birth of the mind and will of God.

I pray that I remain in faith as the promise of God is delivered.

I decree that we (the midwife and the birther) are vessels of faith, and our faith will cause the entry of God's word to be accomplished (Psalms 138:8).

I ask God for wisdom, who gives it liberally, and I pray that the wisdom given will enable me to be a facilitator of the promise (James 1:5).

I pray for the knowledge and wisdom necessary for complicated deliveries (2 Kings 2:10).

I pray that birthers birth the fire of God, and may it be the guiding direction before them (Exodus 13:22).

I pray that those I help in birthing will not grow weary in well-doing (Galatians 6:9).

Your word says that where there are two or more witnesses in agreement, your word is established. May my witness be the confirming sign of that which is to come (2 Corinthians 13:1).

Lord, I ask that the counsel of the Lord falls on me as I counsel others.

Father, take joy in the sacrifice made to bring forth your thoughts and will on the Earth.

Lord, I pray that the glory of the Lord be revealed in our desire to move according to your plans and purposes.

Lord, I pray that our hearts be filled with joy as we expect the goodness of the Lord.

Lord, I pray that my counsel brings confirmation with leaping, just as with Mary and Elizabeth. Father, your word says that obedience is better than sacrifice. May this offering of obedience be acceptable in your sight.

Father, favor us in our time of conception.

Lord, give us faith to continue to cross over into the promise. Let us fight the good fight of faith, and let that place burst forth with milk and honey.

As a facilitator of the promise, I pray that, as a midwife, you give me a distinct plan of action to help others fulfill their God-given assignments. That I will not fear or be dismayed, for God is with me and is my God. He will strengthen me and help me to help others. He will uphold me with His righteous right hand (Isaiah 41:10).

I pray that, as a midwife, you give me the ability to help others birth their future and hope (Jeremiah 29:11).

Lord, you are the sustainer of life, and all things begin and end with you. May your DNA be attached to every birther that I help, and may the glory of the Lord be revealed in my commitment to seeing the work of Christ being established in this seed.

God, allow my words to be the charge that impregnates and sustains the virtue of all those you have given me as assignments and mandates.

May this mind be in all birthers that is also in Christ Jesus (Philippians 2:5).

Lord, grant all birthers foresight, insight, and oversight as they are processing.

I pray that the intellect of God bombards my mind.

I pray for the finances necessary to birth the plans and purposes of God.

FINANCIAL PRAYERS *(as mentioned earlier I would provide)*

I pray that we will be able to go to the fish's mouth to receive abundance in desolation.

I pray that you bless our two fish and five loaves so that there may be an overflow to help the 5,000 in need with abundant leftovers.

Thank you, Lord, for the power to get wealth, and all that is needed for every vision I am pregnant with is provided for out of your riches in glory.

I pray Lord that as you delight in us, you will bring us into the land, and give it us; a land which floweth with milk and honey.

Yes indeed, it won't be long now. Things are going to happen so fast my head will swim, one thing fast on the heels of the other. I won't be able to keep up. Everything will be happening at once—and everywhere I look, blessings! Blessings like wine pouring off the mountains and hills. God will make everything right again for me.
I will rebuild their ruined cities.
I will plant vineyards and drink good wine.
I will work in my gardens and eat fresh vegetables.
And I will plant them, plant them on their own land.

I will never again be uprooted from the land that God has given me.

I will have great resources and intel from God and I will become the marketplace of the nations.

You have crowned my year with goodness and my paths drip in abundance.

I have all things because He spared not his own Son, but delivered him up for us all (Romans 8:32)

I will remember the Lord my God: for it is he that gives me the power to get wealth, that he may establish his covenant which he swore unto my fathers, as it is this day (Deuteronomy 8:18)

The Lord shall open unto me his good treasure, the heaven to give rain unto thy land in his season, and to bless all the work of my hand: and I shalt lend unto many nations, and I shall not borrow. (Duet 28:12)

The blessing of Abraham might come me through Jesus Christ; that I receive the promise of the Spirit through faith (Galatians 3:14)

Christ hath redeemed me from the curse of the law, being made a curse for us: for it is written, cursed is everyone that hangeth on a tree: (Galatians 3:13)

Blessed be the God and Father of our Lord Jesus Christ, who hath blessed me with all spiritual blessings in heavenly places in Christ (Eph 1:3)

I will not stagger at the promises of God through unbelief; but I am strong in faith, giving glory to God; Being fully persuaded that, what he had promised, he is able to perform. (Romans 4:20-21)

I sowed in the land, and reaped in the same year a hundredfold; and the Lord blessed me. I am prospering and continuing to prosper until I become very prosperous (Genesis 26:12-13).

THE BIRTHING PLAN

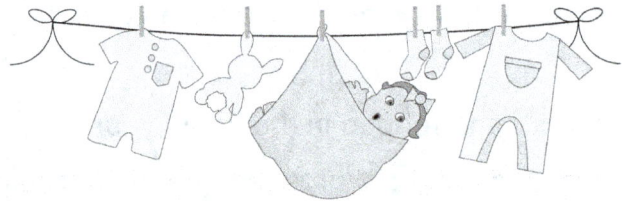

There are day dreams and there are night dreams. Oftentimes when we see a thing, it allows us to enter into a vision. Consider the television, as we see what is on the TV, it allows us to enter into someone's vision they are telling. It is the same with God, we see things all day and when we rest it allows us to enter into the vision God is telling us about what we have seen. We will receive vision in our rest. Meaning, that we come to a place where we are ceasing from work (pushing) and we bring all of our efforts to a moment of pause (resting). When you are in this moment expect day and night dreams. Daydreams are when you go off into an elongated gaze or daze. Pay attention to every look, thought, movement, and vision. This is how you will be able to answer the questions below. This is when we receive vision concerning what God would have us to do or what He would have us to do next.

The Cycle of Vision

(1) Hearing The word

(2) Increasing in faith

(3) See The Word (perception, imagination, experience, envisioning)

(4) Rest

(5) Receive Vision (receive blueprints to proceed)

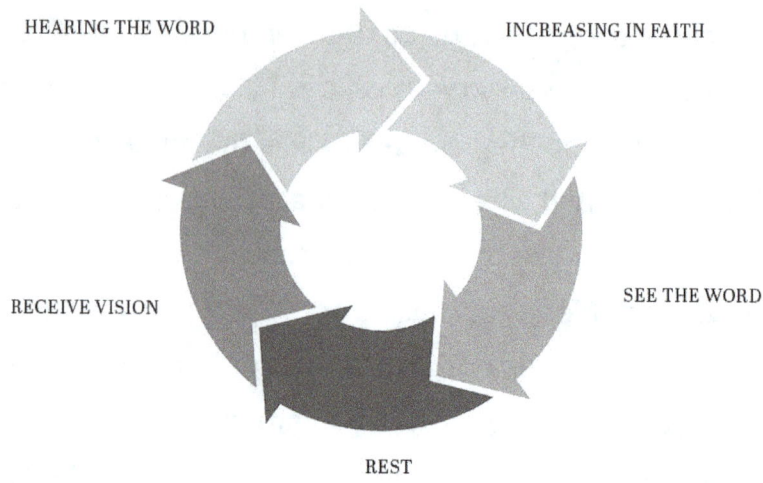

HEARING THE WORD

INCREASING IN FAITH

RECEIVE VISION

SEE THE WORD

REST

May the Lord God grant you the insight and the wisdom to implement His plan. I pray that the anointing of the facilitator of the promise falls upon you and that you experience the free favors of God that shall richly abound to you as you follow His will.

Name:

Date:

Midwife's Name *(this can be God or a friend)*:

Midwife's Phone *(if applicable)*:

Expected Due Date *(declare to God the date by which you want to manifest this promise)*:

Actual Birthdate *(come back and write when the promise manifested)*:

Assignment *(write here the idea, concept, or vision that God has given you)*:

PRE-BIRTH

Environment

Sometimes we don't consider the environment necessary to produce what God has given us. To bring an idea, vision, or concept into the natural realm, we have to determine what the environment looks like. That means what is the environment necessary to produce this idea?

Example: I must have a faith-filled life that consists of daily worship, 1-2 hour prayer time daily, daily confessions, and at least reading 5 chapters of the word daily so that I can have a spirit that is connected to God and able to produce God's word in faith. I need certain resources, 2 managers, 5 employees, a CPA, insurance so on and so forth you get the drift.

Important Background Information

What is the expected outcome of the assignment?

Example: The expected outcome is to be able to have a Fortune 500 company that exists to bring wealth into the Kingdom of God. We desire to become a bank where we loan money to Kingdom entrepreneurs seeking funding for the ideas of God.

Failures (how many times have I failed at producing a result if any?)

Example: I have been waiting for God to heal me and He hasn't done it yet. I have prayed and prayed for years and I still haven't seen the manifestation of my healing so I have had multiple failures. Too many to count.

Where am I angry with God? Where has this emotion stopped me from producing?

Successes (where have I seen the most success if any?)

Example: I was looking to receive deliverance from an elongated battle with sexual addiction and this was one of the successes I had. As I was listening to the word and praying the word, my flesh began to die and I learned the enemy dwells in flesh. One of the books that helped me pray the word was John Eckhart's book, Prayers that Rout Demons. I would pray the scriptures in the book and they were breaking up demonic captivity in my life. As my spirit man became stronger than my fleshy man, meaning I was no longer feeding it more than my spirit, the environment was no longer conducive for the enemy and as I would be in prayer the demons would just come out (self-deliverance).

God has given me the ability to encourage others through the small victories I have had. He has even increased the anointing on my life to bring deliverance to others.

Where am I lacking the confidence to carry out this baby?

Example: (1) I'm not technologically savvy and I don't know how I would acquire clients (2) I'm not sure I could speak in front of people about my product or service.

Write all points where you lack confidence.

DURING BIRTH

What frustrates me in the process of birthing?

Example: I get most frustrated when I gain momentum and the enemy sends a deluge of arrows to distract and keep me from focusing on the promise. I get frustrated with delays; everytime I go to possess a door it is closed to me though I know it was promised to me by God.

What has God mandated me to do that I'm stalling on (having a stillbirth)?

Example: God has told me to have tent revivals and many times I haven't done it because I felt inadequate. I felt like who would I impact? How could I make a mark on the Kingdom in such a small place?

What actions and behaviors do I need to divorce to see to it that this baby can and will be birthed according to its due date?

Example: I need to divorce fear. Many times fear has allowed me to sabotage my destiny because I didn't believe in myself. I would go so far and bow out because I felt like I never had the resources to get the task completed.

What fraction of time in daily life do I need to devote to the birthing of this baby?

How can I gain momentum and keep momentum?

What do I need my midwife to help me the most with?

Two seperate examples:

(1) I need my midwife to aid and assist me with day to day guidance through the transition of grief.

(2) I need my midwife to help me with self deliverance and deliverance exercises that will help me come out of fear and doubt.

POST-BIRTH

What type of after-care is needed to sustain the life of this assignment?

Example: I need bi-weekly accountability calls to deal with matters of uncertainty concerning transition and sustaining momentum. I also need to monthly conduct SWOT analysis so that I recognize my strengths, weaknesses, opportunities and threats so I can keep a proactive approach to sustaining momentum.

CITATIONS

The Bible. King James Version, Bible Gateway, 2026,

   www.biblegateway.com.

Puah: Midrash and Aggadah. (n.d.). Jewish Women's Archive.

   https://jwa.org/encyclopedia/article/puah-midrash-and-agga

   dah

Shiphrah: Midrash and Aggadah. (n.d.). Jewish Women's Archive.

   https://jwa.org/encyclopedia/article/shiphrah-midrash-and-a

   ggadah

STAY CONNECTED

For booking inquiries please reach out to Nikki Garcia Ministries at: (561) 618-8275. You can also email us at nikkigarciaministries@gmail.com or visit us at http://lifegivingrhema.com or https://kingdomgirlnikki.com

View other books written by Nikki Garcia

Join our intercessory prayer Zoom call every Thursday at Midnight
https://tinyurl.com/prayeratmidnight

Sign up for the Office of the Midwife Course Online

https://kingdomacademy.education

Join the conversation and engage with Nikki Garcia

FB, INSTAGRAM, TIKTOK AND YOUTUBE: @kingdomgirlnikki

Click the button below and you can sign up to receive emails whenever Nikki Garcia publishes a new book. There's no charge and no obligation.
https://books2read.com/r/B-A-LSDBB-HVVPC

PRAYER OF SALVATION

Lord God, I am a sinner and I need you in my life. I ask for forgiveness for all of my sins. I confess that Jesus Christ is Lord! I believe in my heart that He is the Son of God and that God raised Him from the dead. Now, Lord, I ask you to come into my heart. Live within me. Dwell within me. My life is no longer my own but I give it to you. I renounce and denounce Satan and his operation in my life and I give you complete control!

If you said this prayer and you meant it which I know you did, then you are now saved!

Let us know you said this prayer by sending an email to:

info@kingdomgirlnikki.com

NOTES

www.ingramcontent.com/pod-product-compliance
Lightning Source LLC
Chambersburg PA
CBHW060347130626
46553CB00003B/1121